MW01641023

# QUOTE ME ON IT

Quote It Till You Know It. Say It Till You See It.

BRENDA L. HARRISON

authorHOUSE®

*AuthorHouse™*
*1663 Liberty Drive*
*Bloomington, IN 47403*
*www.authorhouse.com*
*Phone: 1-800-839-8640*



*Published by AuthorHouse 06/24/2019*

*ISBN: 978-1-4969-6245-4 (sc)*
*ISBN: 978-1-4969-6244-7 (e)*

*Print information available on the last page.*

# Quote Me On It

# Dedication

This book is dedicated to four very special individuals in my life; first, my grandmother, Mattie Lee Polite. She was my best friend, my mentor, my school teacher and so much more. Rest in peace grandmother; I will see you again. To my son, Maurice, who has been there for me through thick and thin. To my daughter, Cortney, for her love and support through the years. I love you guys so much. Last but not least, to the love of my life—Elder Alvin Harrison, my anchor, my friend and my confidant. Thank you for all that you did that enabled me to complete this book. I appreciate God for you and love you so much.

# ACKNOWLEDGEMENTS

I would like to extend a heartfelt thank you to my mother-in-law, Mrs. Dorothy Williams for her prayers, love and support. Thanks to Dawn Alston for her brilliant and creative ideas and for designing my book cover. You are amazing. To my Spelman College family and coworkers: Charlene, Nikki, and Asella: Thank you for your prayers, encouragement, support and enthusiasm. You guys are truly the best. I love being a part of the B&C team. Thanks to my three sisters: Risa, Angie, and Virginia for your love. Thanks, Jasmine Mason for applying my makeup so beautifully so that I would look great for my photo shoot. You did a fabulous job. I am so glad we met. Dan Bascelli thank you so much for your help with the plagiarism and editing piece. Thanks, Sylvia Maddox for connecting me to the right people. Thanks, Melanie Mims Mckie for helping me find one of the best to edit my book. Jenna Ray, thank you for a job well done. Thank you, Nina Scott for the great referrals and for sending Jasmine Mason my way. I was very pleased. My best friend, Cheryl Gamble, you have always celebrated my accomplishments. You have always been supportive, encouraging and so helpful to me in so many ways. Thank you. I love you so much. Thank you, Germaine McAuley, girl you know how to work that camera. Sandra Porter, thank you so much for the referral. I made the right choice. Mr. Terry Johnson and staff with AuthorHouse Publishing, you are a joy to work with.

# CONTENTS

# Foreword

"*Life is a Journey*" most aptly describes the path that led to the birth of this book. It is truly a God inspired project by my wife of 35 years, Brenda Harrison.

In the face of adversities, disappointments, setbacks, losses, health and physical challenges and some things that were just life, Brenda persevered. She never gave up and never stopped believing. She is… and has always been a rock for me along with our two children, Maurice and Cortney. Her *never stop* and *can do it qualities* have been an inspiration to many that know and love her. She works untiringly, loves unconditionally, and never meets a stranger. Throughout the years she has maintained the *blessed assurance,* "I know God is going to do it." Through life experiences, "Quote Me On It" was born. Brenda's prayer, as well as mine is that this book will leave you blessed, inspired, and encouraged. "God is faithful."

With Love, Prayers and Anticipation,
Elder Alvin Harrison

# PREFACE

"Quote Me On It" is one of my greatest inspirations and accomplishments. It is the manifestation of what God can do if you only believe. What inspires me most about this book is the fact that each quote was divinely inspired. I only wrote what I heard, when I heard it from my heavenly father. I am so honored and humbled that he chose to do this through me. You will notice the words – Read, Pause, and Reflect on most pages, which is the definition of the word Selah. My desire is that you will do just that. Quote it till you know it and Say it till you see it manifested in your life. Quote, "I am living everyday under the umbrella of the blessings of God" until it becomes your lifestyle. Say, "I am a book a good read at that" until others see it. Say, "I am living my best life NOW" until it becomes your reality.

# INTRODUCTION

Every quote was divinely inspired. I only wrote what I heard when I heard it from God. It is my desire that these divinely inspired quotes will inspire you as much as they have inspired me.

Quote It Till You Know It. Say It Till You See It.

Read, Pause, Reflect and Apply

## ADVERSITY

**G**reatness is born in the face of adversity. One day greatness will look adversity in the face and say, "Here I am."

**Y**ou can be in trouble, yet not be troubled.

**T**here are some lessons in life we will only learn through adversity.

**I**f you go through, you will come out.

**N**ever doubt God's ability to bring you out.

**G**od can take what appears to be nothing, make something out of it and bless the world with it.

## ATTITUDE

**N**ever allow a bad attitude to rob you of a good day.

**A** winner always wins.

**I**f you change your attitude, God will change your altitude.

## BLESSINGS

**I** live everyday under the umbrella of the blessings of God.

**I**'m living on the other side of through.

**Y**ou've passed the test, now you're ready to be blessed.

**I**f God did it then, he'll do it again.

**I**f you place more emphasis on what you can do for others, your blessings will come quicker.

**T**here is a 5th season: It is your due season.
*–Elder Alvin Harrison*

## CHALLENGES

**Y**ou can challenge the challenge.

**C**hallenges are like crossword puzzles, they are good for the mind.

**Y**our challenge is only an opportunity for growth.

## CHANGE

**T**he Word of God is your blueprint for change.

**B**e the change you want to see in others.

**N**ever underestimate your ability to change.

**W**hile God is working in me, I am working on me.

**C**hange your ways; change your days.

**S**ome things from your past do not fit in your future. –*Elder Alvin Harrison*

## CHARACTER

**I** am a book, a good read at that.

**A** good character will carry you a long way.

## CHOICES

**G**od did not create robots, he created free moral agents.

**C**hoices are only options, choose the right ones.

**Y**ou have the power to choose.

## COMMUNICATION

**C**ommunication is the C in the ABC's of Marriage.

**E**ffective communication is the prerequisite to understanding.

**C**ommunication is the key that opens the door to good relationships.

**B**ad communication corrupts good conversation.

**S**ometimes the answer you get depends on whom you ask. Ask the wrong person get the wrong answer. Ask the right person get the right answer. Know your source. –*Elder Alvin Harrison*

## COMPASSION

**W**hen you hurt, I care.

**C**ompassion is a great act of kindness.

## DEATH

**S**eemingly, some are more appreciated dead than alive.

**L**ive the sermon you would like to have preached at your funeral.

**M**ay your life be the greatest sermon ever preached.

**I**f you want something to die, stop feeding it. – *Elder Alvin Harrison*

## DECISIONS

The decision you make today could affect someone else tomorrow.

The choices made today will determine the consequences you face tomorrow.

## DEPRESSION

Depression is a state of mind that we should never embrace.

When depression knocks, don't answer.

To blessed to be stressed and depressed.

## DETERMINATION

Do not stop until you reach the top; when you get there reach down and pull someone else up with you.

The secret is not convincing others that you can, but convincing yourself that you can.

## DIRECTION

Hear God then move, but do not move until you hear God.

God is my spiritual GPS Navigator.

If you follow God's direction, you will never get lost.

## ENTHUSIASM

Enthusiasm is contagious, catch it.

Enthusiasm is not popular.

## EXCELLENCE

The norm is too normal, be excellent.

## EXCUSES

Excuses will rob you of great opportunities.

## EXPECTATION

Expectation gives birth to fulfillment. *–Elder Alvin Harrison*

I'm expecting to live and I'm living expecting. *–Elder Alvin Harrison*

## EXPERIENCES

If you listen to the voice of experience, you won't have to repeat the test.

## FAILURE

Defeat has been defeated.

Perseverance is my choice, failure is not.

## FAITH

When God sees faithfulness he sees a reflection of himself. *–Elder Alvin D. Harrison*

Faith is seeing what others don't and doing what others won't.

## FAVOR

Favor can be your best friend, the lack of it your worse enemy.

If you want God's attention, give him yours.

## FEAR

Honor man, fear God.

**F**ear paralyzes, it makes one immobile.

**D**on't worry about people knowing who you are. Do you know who you are?

## FORGIVENESS

**U**nforgiveness is venomous.

**F**orgiveness is like a breath of fresh air, so refreshing.

**T**he forgiven forgives.

## FRIENDS

**B**e one of the best things that ever happened to someone else.

**A** true friend will keep your secrets.

**B**e the kind of friend that you would like to have.

**F**riends, if you get a dozen worth a dime that's good.

## GOD

**H**ow do I spell God? Love.
**H**ow do I spell Love? God.



READ . PAUSE . REFLECT . APPLY

**G**od is the greatest pain killer I know.

**Y**ou can't complete me, only God can. I am complete in him.

**W**hen we work with God, then all things will work.
*– Elder Alvin Harrison*

## GROWTH

**Y**ou can bloom right where you are.

**Y**ou are never too small to grow.

## HEALTH

**Y**ou can't enjoy your wealth when your in bad health.

## HOLINESS

**H**oliness is never wrong.

**G**od never changed his mind concerning holiness. Man did.

**H**oliness is wholeness.

## HONOR

**H**onor someone other than yourself.
**H**onor is such an honorable thing to do.

## HOPE

**H**old on to hope or become hopeless.

## HUMILITY

**I**'m humble because I realize who I am and know who God is.

**H**umility is the realization that I can't do anything without him, but he can do anything without me.

## INFLUENCE

**M**y greatest influence is the word of God.

**L**ive a life that will influence others long after you're gone.

**I**nfluence family first.

## INTEGRITY

Integrity is not what you do—it's who you are, a person of integrity.

What you do defines who you are, if only for that moment.

## JEALOUSY

Always celebrate the blessings of others: Yours will come.

You hinder your blessings when you are jealous of the blessings of others.

Don't be a hater; be a celebrator.

## KNOWLEDGE

What you have knowledge of has now become your responsibility.

Knowledge is a cake, wisdom is the icing on it.

The wise know what to do with what he knows.

Knowledge is not always against you, it is also in your favor. Use it.

**LIFE**

**D**on't allow your past to paralyze your future.
**L**eave the past in the past.
**I**'m living a good life in bad times.
**L**ive your better life **NOW.**
**T**here is a better life with your name on it.
**L**ive the sermon you would like to have preached at your funeral.

**W**ho you were depended on you, who you are depends on you, and who you will be is depending on you. – *Elder Alvin Harrison*

**LISTEN**

**L**ord put a hush in my spirit so that I will know when it is time to be quiet.

**L**isten for what's not being said.

**Y**ou can't see what I'm saying if you didn't hear what I said. – *Elder Alvin Harrison*

**LOVE**

**D**on't treat people the way they treat you; when you do – you become that person.

**L**ove will build a bridge; in other words, you will find a way to get over it.

**A**re you walking love or talking love?

## MINISTRY

**Y**our misery might just be your ministry.
**G**od will turn your mess into a message.

## MIRACLES

**M**iracles still happen.
**M**iracles are not for sale.

## MOTIVATION

**M**otivation is nothing without determination.

## OPINIONS

**S**omeone else's opinion is someone else's opinion.
**Y**our opinion is your opinion.

## OPPORTUNITIES

**O**ne opportunity can change your entire life.
**G**reat opportunities don't come around everyday.
**W**hen opportunity calls, answer the phone.
**W**hen opportunity knocks, answer the door.

## PEACE

**T**he side effect of peace is peace.
**Y**ou can't put a price tag on peace.
**I** believe enough has a lifespan, so when is enough enough.

## PERFECTION

**T**rue perfection has no boundaries and a man is limited only by himself. – *Elder Alvin Harrison*

## PERSEVERANCE

**P**erseverance is my choice, quitting is never an option.

**B**elieve in your dreams, pursue your passion and God will make it happen.

**Y**ou can't complete your assignment and receive a passing grade doing nothing.

## POTENTIAL

**D**on't be an almost made it with an extraordinary potential. – *Elder Alvin Harrison*

## PRAISE

If we can't praise him for where we are, then we must praise him from where we are – *Elder Alvin Harrison*

## PROGRESSION

Sometimes in life in order to get where you're trying to go; you have to go where you've never been.

## PROSPERITY

Prosperity becomes destruction in the hands of a fool.

## PURPOSE

It's very important in this season that you tap into your earthly purpose.

You are here on purpose.
God intentionally created you.
You are not a mistake.

## RELIGIOUS

**M**any are religious, but few are righteous.

## REJECTION

**T**he spirit of rejection is heavy upon us, but we must not let it weigh us down.

**R**emove the last three letters from the word rejection. That's not who you are.

## RHYTHM

**F**inding the rhythm is finding how you flow.
**W**e serve a God of rhythm.
**F**low with the rhythm of God.
**T**he silence of the rhythm is just as important as the sound.

**I**'ve found my rhythm.
**Y**ou must have an ear to hear the rhythm.
**R**hythm is made of sound and silence.
**T**he silence is a part of the rhythm.

## SILENCE

**B**ecause it's silent doesn't mean God is ignoring you.



READ . PAUSE . REFLECT . APPLY

**B**ecause you don't hear God doesn't mean he is not speaking.

**G**od is moving even in the silence.

## SOLITUDE

**S**ometimes it's good to be alone.

## STEWARDSHIP

**G**od expects us to be good stewards of everything that he has entrusted us with.

## SUCCESS

**Y**ou don't have to wait for an invitation to succeed, just take a step in the right direction. – *Elder Alvin Harrison*

**I**f you are good, strive to become better, if you are great, strive to become greater. Never quit, never stop until you attain success. – *Elder Alvin Harrison*

**S**uccess does not come in a day, but it comes based on what you do daily. – *Elder Alvin Harrison*

## TEMPTATION

When tempted, don't yield.

## THOUGHTS

One thought can be worth a million dollars.
Thoughts are ideas and ideas are thoughts.

When someone says something to you that you don't like; take the time to examine its validity.

It is sad when you are neither offensive nor defensive, when you don't fight for or against anything. – *Elder Alvin Harrison*

## TIME

God will take time out of the equation. –*Elder Al Harrison*

God's time matters most.
Time spent unwisely can never be recaptured.
We must learn how to be better stewards of time.
Sometimes you have to run while others walk. –
*Elder Alvin Harrison*

## TITHING

It's so interesting how the enemy makes the 10% seem so large and the 90% seem so small.

God said bring the first fruits, not the last.

Tithing works, work it.

## TRUST

When worry knocks, send trust to the door.

Either you worry or you trust, it's impossible to do both simultaneously.

Worry out, trust in.
Faith can chase a problem and put worry to flight.

Trust says, "I believe I can do it," faith says, "I know I can."

## UNITY

The first three letters in the word unity **U N I** defines what it is.

## VALUE

The quality and worth of who you are is greater than you can imagine.

Your value will make room for you and make you desirable to others.

God always saw you as a person of value.
Don't allow people to put you on their scale of worth and appraise the value of who you are.

The worth of a thing is not in its price, but it is in the one who thinks it is priceless. – *Elder Alvin Harrison*

You were a gem even in the junk.

See yourself the way God see you and that is a person of value and worth.

You've never been a nothing or a nobody, only a work in progress.

Don't let what you are going through cause you to lose your sense of worth.

Don't allow people to give the benediction for your life. God has the last say.

## VICTORY

**O**ne victory is not enough when we have many battles to fight. – *Elder Alvin Harrison*

## WAIT

**G**od anoint us to handle the weight of the wait. **W**hat appears to be too long for you is not too late for God.

**Y**our situation can change at any given moment. What a difference a day makes.

**L**et Waiting Work.

## WILL

**G**od's will is his original mind and intent for mankind. –*Elder Alvin Harrison.*

**I**f you want to know what the will of God is for your life, you can find it in his word.

**M**y will is his will and his will is my will.

## WISDOM

Wisdom is knowing what to do with what you know.

Wisdom makes one wise.

Wisdom sometimes says no, not now, wait or later
Wisdom is something you should never say no to.
When wisdom knocks, answer.

## WORDS

Words uttered cannot be retrieved.
What you say about others, others will say about you.

Words are like still water, they run deep.

## WORRY

Cast your worries upon him then wait on him.
When worry knocks, trust answers.
Either you worry or you trust. It's impossible to do both simultaneously.

Worry out, trust in.

Some worry sometimes, most worry all of the time.



READ . PAUSE . REFLECT . APPLY

**I**f we immerse ourselves in what God has called us to do, we won't have time to worry about what others are doing.

## WORSHIP

**W**orship is greater than a feeling or an expression. It is an experience.

**I**s he worth your worship?

**Y**ou become a worshipper when your worship becomes you.

# THE 12 NEVER STOPS

Never stop loving God.
Never stop loving yourself.
Never stop loving people.
Never stop trusting God.
Never stop forgiving.
Never stop crying, (Jesus wept); it
shows that you have compassion.
Never stop walking in integrity.
Never stop speaking the truth in love.
Never stop working on the man
or woman in the mirror.
Never stop helping others.
Never stop ministering to others.
Never stop living holy.

# YOUR GIFT

God has blessed each of us with gifts and talents to be utilized for his glory. Your gift was handed to you at birth and flourished in you as a child; unfortunately, in many instances it went unnoticed. In what area(s) are you naturally proficient and excellent? What is it that you find yourself doing that you have a passion for? What is it that you would do without compensation? Your gift is not cumbersome nor is it difficult to perform. It is easy because it is your God given gift. You could do it with your eyes closed. Your gift is very exciting. You could actually see yourself making a career out of it because God has equipped you to handle it. Your gift should always shine; therefore, you must keep it polished and never allow it to get rusty or dusty. Your gift will set you in large places and introduce you to the world. Always use it.

# TO HOW MANY ARE YOU ASSIGNED?

In Exodus the 18th chapter, Moses' father in law Jethro advised him of a better plan because what Moses was undertaking was too much for him alone. Jethro instructed his father in law as follows:

Exodus 18:17 Jethro said to Moses: "The thing that thou doest is not good."

Exodus 18:18 For this thing is too heavy for thee; thou art not able to perform it thyself alone.

Exodus 18:19 Hearken now unto my voice, I will give thee counsel and God shall be with thee: Be thou for the people to God-ward that thou mayest bring the causes unto God:

Exodus 18:20 And thou shalt teach them ordinances and laws and shalt shew them the way wherein they must walk and the work that they must do.

Exodus 18:21 Moreover thou shalt provide out of all the people able men such as fear God, men of truth, hating covetousness; place such over them to be rulers of thousands, and rulers of hundreds (rulers of fifties and rulers of tens):

# To How Many Are You Assigned?

Exodus 18:22 And let them judge the people at all seasons: and it shall be that every great matter they shall bring unto thee, but every small matter they shall judge: so shall it be easier for thyself and they shall bear the burden with thee.

Now here is the key; Exodus 18:21 - Some of them were rulers of fifties and some of them were rulers of tens. Your assignment might be to ten. I know we don't want to accept that, but listen; everyone is not assigned to the masses. Do not worry about how many members you have? Do not compare yourself to other ministries? Embrace what God has given you. Take those ten and let the Lord use you to help transform the lives of those ten and train them to do likewise. You will be amazed to see what God can do with ten. God said in Matthew 18:20 - For where two or three are gathered together in my name, there am I in the midst of them. Thank you for this Word of wisdom Apostle Roscoe Willis.

# Renew a Right Spirit Within Me

**Psalms 51: 10** - Create in me a clean heart, O God; and renew a right spirit within me.

We should all desire a right spirit. It is a right spirit that causes us to love those that don't love us. It is a right spirit that causes us to render kind deeds to those that won't say "thank you." It is a right spirit that causes you to forgive when you know you did no wrong. It is a right spirit that causes you to forgive and let it go. It is a right spirit that nudges you, telling you to be quiet when you want to say something negative about someone. It is a right spirit that causes you to continuously strive to please God and make him happy.

# Be Grateful

Every time you laugh, someone cries.
Every time you eat, someone is hungry.
Every time you wake up, someone sleeps away.
Every time you look at your children, someone wishes they could do the same.
Every time you complain about your job, someone would gladly take it.
Every time you look at your spouse in anger, someone wishes they could see theirs just one more time.
Every time you complain about walking up and down steps, someone would gladly do so if they had legs.
Every time you get angry because you are short on cash, someone has no cash at all.
Every time you complain about not earning enough money on your job, someone wish they had a job.
Every time you complain because you don't like the car you drive, someone is walking to the bus stop.
Every time you throw food away, someone would have loved to have your leftovers.
Every time you complain about how much housework you have, someone wishes they had a place to call home.
Every time you feel a little nudge of pain, someone's body racks with pain.
Every time you get angry because you feel you deserve so much more in life, someone wishes they had what you already have.

# Let Waiting Work

Waiting is something that we're all familiar with. When the wait is long it can become quite frustrating. This is when the hours become days, the days become weeks, the weeks become months and the months become years. The scripture states, "Let patience have her perfect work." Let is the key word here. How do I let waiting work? How do I do that when I've been waiting for seemingly a lifetime and nothing seems to be changing in my life? Well, you must wait with the right spirit; if you wait angrily because you think God has done you an injustice that will only extend the wait. A few years ago I was in a very unpleasant situation. I went through it for three years. I was angry, having a pity party, but nothing changed until I took the focus off of my situation and placed it on God. I started thanking God in the place that I was in; not *for* it, but *in* it. I was totally delivered out of it, but not until I changed my attitude. When I changed my attitude, God changed my altitude. "Wait on the Lord; be strong and let your heart take courage - Psalms 27:14. There goes that word let again. While we wait we must be strong. Now, that strength comes from God alone, knowing that our God is a promise keeper and that good things come to those that wait. You must know that a change will come, and it will. This is called confidence. Knowing is how we let patience work. I know I will get through this. The second part of that scripture says, "Let your heart take courage." You must take courage right where you are.

# Let Waiting Work

Only God can help you do this. Waiting silently - Psalms 62:1-5 - My soul, wait in silence for God. Sometimes we have to wait in silence. We have to tell our emotions to shut up. Stop talking about what you are going through and start talking and working on what you are going to.

# Rules for a Better Life

*Love God and live for Him. Live HOLY. *Love your
spouse. Treat them better than you treat anyone else.
*Love your family and friends. Show it, if
you don't show it; they won't know it.
*Forgive those that hurt you.
*Exercise, rest, eat right and take care your body.
*Keep people out of your business.
*Learn to let people go when they
don't want you in their life.
*Treat people the way you would
like for them to treat you.
*Laugh, have fun, enjoy life.
*Don't be selfish always find yourself
helping the hurting.
*Don't forget about the widows and the elderly.
*Don't be envious and jealous of others.
This hinders your blessings.
*Speak kind words about and to others.
*Don't be a busybody, nosy and prying.
*Be careful who you let in your inner circle.
*Sometimes it's just good to be alone,
spending quality time with yourself.
*Know that you don't know everything.
Age has nothing to do with it.
*Learn to be quite sometimes. You don't have
to say something about everything.
*Believe in yourself. Don't settle.
*Do what God has chosen you to do.

*Don't let people control you.
*It's ok to say NO sometimes.
*Don't be controlling. People don't like being around that type spirit.
*Don't provoke your children. Learn where to draw the line.
*Respect
*Don't be overly sensitive. Learn to ignore people.
*Stay focused and continue moving forward.
*Be the kind of person that people love to be around.

## Confidence vs. Arrogance

Confidence is a strong form of belief. Belief in who you are, your abilities, even your purpose. You don't need a college degree to have it. You are a person of worth with or without a college degree. It's very important that you know that. When you truly have confidence in yourself you are not intimidated by others because you know who you are.

Arrogance is the offensive display of superiority or self-importance and overbearing pride according to the freedictionary.com. Most times people do not enjoy the company of those who are arrogant. Most enjoy the company of those who are confident because you glean and learn so much from them. Arrogant individuals are usually very irritating, selfish and head strong. Arrogance is very distasteful in the sight of God. It is synonymous with pride and a proud look which is one of the things God hates according to the holy scriptures.

## NOTES

## NOTES

## NOTES

# NOTES

## NOTES

# NOTES

# About the Author:

Brenda Harrison was born in Smithfield, North Carolina. She earned a Master's degree in Organization and Management with a specialization in Human Resource Management from Capella University in 2006. She furthered her studies by entering the Ph.D. program at Capella, studying Training and performance improvement. In undergraduate studies she earned a B.S. degree in Organizational Management from Claflin University. Brenda had the honor of presenting for the Women of Excellence Leadership Series at Spelman College in 2005. Her presentation and talk was entitled "The Art of Leadership."

She noticed the ability and passion for writing quotes while serving as assistant pastor with her husband at "Manifested Destiny Ministries" in McDonough, Georgia. All quotes written by Brenda were divinely inspired. It has become one of her greatest passions.

Her motto is: Perseverance is my choice, quitting is not an option.

Made in the USA
Columbia, SC
06 September 2019